This Little Poem

This Little Poem

Seb Doubinsky

LEAKY BOOT PRESS

This Little Poem
by Seb Doubinsky

First published in 2015 by
Leaky Boot Press
http://www.leakyboot.com

Copyright © 2015 Seb Doubinsky
All rights reserved

No part of this book may be reproduced or transmitted in any form or by any means, electronic, mechanical, photocopying, recording, or otherwise, without prior written permission of the author.

ISBN: 978-1-909849-17-4

Special thanks

To all my Facebook friends who made this series reach its goal, which was to give back poetry its rank as a "minor genre."

this poem refuses to be beautiful
this poem refuses to speak about beauty
this poem wants to be considered
just as a poem and nothing else

This Little Poem

this poem got a full tank
a cleaned windshield
and air in the tires
this poem can drive long

this poem has no metaphor
no image no allegory
this poem has nothing
hidden or mysterious
this poem is actually
a sculpture a painting
a photograph or a shoe or a hat

This Little Poem

this poem went to the market
this poem went to church
this poem went to war
this poem went to a demonstration
and this little poem
bought an image
and pinned it on its wall

this poem doesn't believe
in poetry anymore
it thinks it is vain
pointless and limited
this poem, like Rimbaud in Aden,
wants to stop being written

This Little Poem

this poem wants a cat
many beautiful poems
have cats in them
but not this one
not even a bird

this poem is a translation
but it doesn't know that
it thinks it is the original
but no, it isn't
it is a palimpsest of itself

This Little Poem

this poem is 100% artificial
absolutely no natural images,
sugar or color added

this poem has beautiful horns
its skull radiates in the dark
it is a demon poem of fear and beauty
but remember: this poem
is only a projection
of yourself

This Little Poem

this poem is loved by
Apollo, Aphrodite and Hermes
this poem has temples in Greece
this poem is a tough motherfucker

Seb Doubinsky

this poem loves love
sweet metaphors
and older poems
this poem is looking for
a soul-mate with
the same interests
if possible

This Little Poem

this poem is a funny
little cracked object
sitting on my shelf
it is completely useless
and gathers dust
I think I will keep it
for a little while longer
though—you never know
it might become useful
one day

Seb Doubinsky

you will find this poem
sitting every day
under the olive tree
eating a couple of figs
if you sit next to it
it will tell you things
you won't be able to understand
because it lost all its teeth
a long time ago
still it has a nice voice
and the figs taste good

This Little Poem

this poem always improvises
the audience often throws things
at it but it doesn't care
it is part of its improvisation

this poem is a love dynamo
see it shake its little behind
and move to the music
it knows the lyrics of all the songs
of course: it wrote them all

This Little Poem

this poem thinks
that poets are
extraordinary people
it obviously
has never
met one

Seb Doubinsky

this poem was published
in the New Yorker once
it talks about it all the time
and all the time and all the time
it doesn't stop to smoke a cigarette
chat with its neighbors
or enjoy the passing of seasons
it just talks all the time
alone in its big paper apartment

This Little Poem

this poem doesn't think
it means anything
but it isn't sure
to be a poem can be
so confusing at times
so it combs its hair
looking at itself in the mirror
wondering if other people
see the same thing
as what it sees

this poem likes to travel
it speaks many languages
and has three pairs of sunglasses
still it never tans and remains
as white as a paper page

This Little Poem

this poem likes the sound of the rain
knocking on the window pane
with its child-like fingers
the wind that combs the trees
and the clouds that disappear
like poems about to be written

this poem thinks it's Jewish
but isn't sure—it might be
Muslim, gypsy or gay
it might even be a woman or
a nine year old working in a textile factory
this poem could be anything
with a sad story to tell
but it sure has a big nose

(for Matthew Lippman)

This Little Poem

this poem is this poem and nothing else
no wannabee, no philosopher, no priest
no hipster, no dark-eyed sailor, no magician
"what you see is what you get"
exactly—and it keeps being the poem
waving proudly its tiny ID
when it knocks on your door

this poem is proud to be gay
not proud proud as to play the trumpet
and dance outside naked in the rain
but proud enough to tell that other poem
that it's beautiful no matter what other people say

This Little Poem

this poem is caught between
the four walls of the sun
and looks out the window
hoping for some wind
and the melody
of the ice-cream van

Seb Doubinsky

this poem lost its job
it has no money nor any clean shirts
it will rhyme for food, shelter and a tiny guitar

This Little Poem

this poem is smoking its pipe
outside looking at the stars
the sky is the largest crossroad
and the most perplexing
the poem lights its pipe again
sitting on its porch
watching a plane
blink and blink and blink again
until it disappears into the warm summer night

this poem loves sunsets
because they remind it
of happy endings and couples
walking hand in hand
on the beach
sunrises on the other hand
remind it of bad hangovers
and the dog breath
of another weird day
full of empty images

This Little Poem

this poem doesn't exist
it is just a few words
a lightning
a sketch
a desire
this

don't tell this poem it is not an poem
it has bought a collection of lovely clothes
just to go out and be a poem
so don't be mean and invite it
to sit at your table if you see it
wandering sadly in front of your café
with its shiny shoes, pastel shirt and strange hat

This Little Poem

this poem believes poetry is the Multiverse
quantum images, distant metaphor clusters
repeated infinitely in different melodies
creating beautiful skies, new universes
and heartbroken sighs

this poem is so short
it could be a haiku
but it is Catholic

This Little Poem

this poem has nothing to say
so it will just mime it

this poem has a paper crown
it weighs nothing but shines under the sun
as this poem pushes its empty cart
in the noisy morning streets

This Little Poem

this poem has only three coins in its pocket
but it's more than enough:
they are eternal, like its pocket

this poem is a snob
it only likes poems like itself
it is too long although it is rather short
all its friends are snobs too
they love to get together and be boring
laughing at the other poems
having a party downstairs

This Little Poem

sun bakes sky
sky reflects roofs
this poem goes to work
its shirt sticking to its back

this poem is no pope
no shaman no rabbi nor imam
this poem has no soul no halo
no special powers
it's just a little poem
who welcomes strangers
with a glass of water, a little song
and a few bills should they have nowhere to stay
it's just a little poem some are glad to know
and who simply shrugs when asked why
there is no lock on its door

This Little Poem

this poem reads the paper every morning
then folds it neatly and puts in at the bottom
of its bird-cage because it knows
birds need fresh news every day

this poem is an atheist
it doesn't believe in poetry

This Little Poem

this poem is a powerful demon
with charcoal eyes, a flaming tongue
and red-hot steel claws
it is the demon of poetry
which can, like fire,
warm your frozen hands
or burn your house down
just because it can

Seb Doubinsky

this poem hates competitions
because it knows that no one
can win or lose in poetry
—birds sing only because
they are their songs

This Little Poem

this poem is buying groceries
it has a list that reminds it
of a Ginsberg list
that was put to auction once
this poem wonders if the buyer
bought the same things
and made a poem
out of it

don't ask this poem where it's going
because it doesn't know and doesn't care
it was a ship once and a bird and the wind
now it is just a poem wandering round
enjoying its hard-earned freedom

This Little Poem

this poem is very difficult to understand
it mumbles all the time

this poem drank a lot of absinth
in its younger days
and fought with Van Gogh and the devil
today it drinks pastis and fights
with no one except
the ghosts of its youth
who always seem to win
ah the trembling hands
the watery eyes
and the sweet licorice breath

(for John Cunningman Egan)

This Little Poem

this poem is an alchemist and a banker
and a gangster and a dragon and a witch
you can't kill it but if you can find it
it might bring you love,
a pack of smokes
and a pair of aces

this poems sings little songs
it alone remembers
sometimes the birds sing them too
turning them into ephemeral symphonies

 ## This Little Poem

this poem is a clone of this poem

Seb Doubinsky

this poem sits under the tree
happily farting
and watching the frogs
hop into the pond

This Little Poem

this poem is back from vacation
it got a nice tan and a few mosquito bites
it can speak a few more languages too
and is thinking about getting a translation of itself
tattooed on its arm soon

this poem is on the road
a little cloud of dust in the rear-mirror
growing bigger every second
until it passes you with a deafening roar
but then you see nothing but a little cloud of dust
this time growing smaller every second
heading straight for the checkered flag of the sun

This Little Poem

this poem is walking in the rain
it doesn't think about getting wet though
it thinks about writing a novel

Seb Doubinsky

this poem looks at itself
in the night window
blurred portrait with a few moths
a tiny moon and a disappearing car
ah the flatness of the self

This Little Poem

do not trust this poem
it will invite you to its place
pour a drug into your drink
steal all your images
and replace them
with second-hand metaphors

this poem loves second-hand poetry
it smells a little bit of dust and love
and is so nicely worn down
that it fits perfectly

This Little Poem

this poem whispers to the ear of the dead
it takes their hands and strokes them gently
in the dark cinema of their super 8 memories
reading the subtitles out loud
so they can follow their long forgotten plot

this poem is not that poem
it is very annoyed
when people mix them up
that poem is sold-out plastic pop culture
whereas this poem is pure white marble
even if it does look like plastic from a distance

This Little Poem

this poem takes no prisoners
except those who want to be taken
it calls them "readers"
and frees them hastily
as they become annoying very fast

Seb Doubinsky

this poem walks barefoot
it likes the feeling of dust
under its paper-white toes
and the aura of fake holiness
that makes the cars slow down
and the birds sing louder

This Little Poem

this poem has three silver coins in its pocket
to pay Charon should he ever have to cross the
Acheron
of course it is immortal but one cannot be sure
anymore

this poem is drinking beers with this other poem
they both cry on their lost loves and laugh at
      their lost fist-fights
they display their new tattoos and tip generously
these two poems are handsome losers in a city
      of winners

This Little Poem

this poem never went to school
never learned anything
never got a diploma
this poem's hands are hard and dry
its back twisted from hard work
its eyes see through shallow images
and it can tell when you're speaking
of what you know not
this poem is not stupid nor wise
it only takes its time before it answers
if it chooses to answer

this poem has an image problem
all the mirrors are either too big or too small
and the windows all open on a fixed landscape
it thinks about quitting and becoming something else
like a reader, an academic or a defrocked preacher
—something with no responsibilities attached
and an illusion of power

This Little Poem

this poem sits on the ledge of the bridge
looking down at the large river
some people are afraid it will jump or fall
but it is not here to end its days
it watches the fish swim among the clouds
and its own transparent reflection
which shows who it really is

this poem neither likes, comments, promotes or shares
this poem is not on Facebook
this poem doesn't have to wear dark glasses
lie about its age, or worry about private pictures
this poem doesn't care about the world out there
this poem only exists because it wants to
by the incredible power of its non-rhyming will

This Little Poem

this poem fears nothing
not even its own shadow
well if it had a shadow
that is

this little poem is lying in the grass
looking at something we can't really see
but know it's there or at least
we want to be there
—like a memory of ourselves
a useless absolution
or a long awaited comfort

This Little Poem

this poem is single
it has no income
no house no car
no TV no dog no children
not a single thing to offer
not even a title

Seb Doubinsky

this poem knows its classics
Homer, Virgil, Li Bai, Ronsard,
Lucky Strike, Pontiac, absinth and opium

This Little Poem

this poem is invisible
you only see it when
it passes in front of another poem

Seb Doubinsky

this poem stutters
but its images
are b-b-b-beautiful

This Little Poem

this poem collects images of butterflies
pins them down cautiously and puts them in
    glass boxes
and admires them until their colors fade and the
    paper wrinkles
—that's how this poem sees itself and it makes it sigh

Seb Doubinsky

this poem paints its nails
singing softly sad love songs
that makes it both cry and giggle

This Little Poem

this poem counts its money
three gold coins and a silver one
gold for the bad days
silver for the good ones

this poem creaks like old wood
laughs like polished metal
and smells of a very old cologne
this poem can tell you stories
if you ever take your time to sit with it
and wait for the tea to brew

This Little Poem

this poem is homeless
but it will gladly share its cardboard house with you
the few cents it has collected and the warmth of its
cheap wine
I said it was homeless
I didn't say it was heartless

(for Jerry Wilson)

this poem is not like this poem
no no no
this poem is like this poem

This Little Poem

this poem tastes like chicken

this poem refuses to judge
it has many opinions though
and will share them gladly
but it will never judge you them or itself
too many are already doing that

This Little Poem

this poem is not the poet
this poem is not seb doubinsky
for instance
no not at all

this poem is a true revolutionary
it keeps moving forward
only stopping to pee
or to admire a flower by the side of the road
or to speak with a baby in a carriage
or to see and old black and white film in a
        rundown theater
or to read a good book
or to go out and drink with good friends
it keeps moving forward though
at its own pace, its black and red flag carefully
folded in its pocket, ready to be waved
when it has finally arrived

(to Niall McDevitt)

This Little Poem

this poem is extremely long
but you have to see it from above

this poem is a little sad
like a half-eaten apple
or a mouth shut before speaking
nothing serious
nothing serious
nothing to rhyme about

(For Justin Grimbol)

This Little Poem

this poem is so crazy
it thinks it's prose

this poem refuses to judge
it has many opinions though
and will share them gladly
but it will never judge you them or itself
too many are already doing that

This Little Poem

this poem likes small things
like new words a change in the season
diamonds pearls or sapphires
it isn't picky
they just have to be small
beautiful and useless

(for Deral F. Fenderson)

this poem has a hangover
this poem shouldn't be recited too loud

This Little Poem

this poem has a few tattoos and many scars
many think they're metaphors
but they're wrong
they just don't know
how to read skin

(for Dominic Albanese and Alicia Young)

Seb Doubinsky

this poem is an object in itself
yet it is unbreakable
doesn't collect dust
and is weightless
like the night, breath and dreams

This Little Poem

this poem doesn't believe in genres
categories or classifications
it only believes in good sex, good drinking
and good friends, not necessarily in that order
of course

Seb Doubinsky

this poem is on facebook
twitter and ello
this poem is very connected
but doesn't share much
it is just curious about
the illusory power
of electricity

This Little Poem

this poem is watching the rain
thinking about being a poem
about watching the rain

this poem is blinded by the sun
this poem is like us in many ways
it knows the danger of beauty
but faces it nonetheless

This Little Poem

this poem comes this poem goes
this poem is like a melody of itself
forgotten then remembered then forgotten again
like the song of the wind the glow of the moon
and the smile on your face

this poem is like a scratched record
this poem is like a scratched record
this poem is...
(silence)
(silence)

This Little Poem

this poem is a fraud
a palimpsest a copy
this poem has stolen everything
from many other poems
and doesn't care
this poem is a con-artist
that all the other poems envy
and try to imitate

(For J-M. Apostolides)

this poem is sick and tired of being nice
this poem wants to be evil
and mean and dangerous
this poem wants to be respected
as bitches are respected
and nothing less

This Little Poem

this poem is trying to look like a round object
but keeps changing shape, color and skin
making it difficult to hold or look at
although it tastes great
as it rolls on your tongue

this poem watches the winter morning
change from black to gray
it feels the color of ink bonds them
in a curiously moving way

This Little Poem

this poem is sitting by itself at the bar
no, it doesn't need company
but if you wish, you can put another coin
in the jukebox and play that same song again
the one that makes think of all the other poems
you once knew or you wish you'd known

www.ingramcontent.com/pod-product-compliance
Lightning Source LLC
LaVergne TN
LVHW041547070426
835507LV00011B/974